A CLASS OF THEIR OWN

Plants

Flowering Plants, Ferns, Mosses, and Other Plants

By
Shar Levine
Leslie Johnstone

Crabtree Publishing Company
www.crabtreebooks.com

Crabtree Publishing Company

www.crabtreebooks.com

Authors: Shar Levine, Leslie Johnstone
Series consultant: Sally Morgan, MA, MSc, MIBiol
Project director: Ruth Owen
Designer: Alix Wood
Editors: Mark Sachner, Adrianna Morganelli
Proofreader: Molly Aloian
Project manager: Kathy Middleton
Production coordinator: Katherine Berti
Prepress technician: Katherine Berti

Developed & Created by R∪bʏ Tuesdaʏ Books Ltd

Front cover: The leaves of an agave plant

Title page: Tulips are members of the Liliaceae, or Lily, family.

Photographs:
Yong Cai, Ph.D: page 25 (all)
FLPA: pages 4 (top), 4 (main), 6, 7 (row 1, right), 7 (row 2, left),
7 (row 2, right), 7 (row 4, left), 7 (row 4, right), 7 (row 5, left),
7 (row 5, right), 7 (bottom), 8 (left), 8 (right), 9 (top), 11 (top),
11 (center), 13 (top), 14 (top left), 15 (top center), 15 (bottom right),
16, 18, 20, 21 (left), 23 (top), 23 (bottom), 24 (right), 24 (left),
27 (inset), 28 (main), 29, 30, 33 (top left), 33 (top center),
33 (bottom), 36, 37 (main), 38 (top), 38 (center), 41 (top), 42 (bottom)
Shar Levine: pages 1, 17, 24 (top), 28 (top), 40 (main), 41 (bottom left),
43 (main)
Redfern Natural History: page 39
Ruby Tuesday Books Ltd: page 32
Science Photo Library: pages 10, 13 (bottom), 14, 24 (bottom),
27 (main)
Shutterstock: front cover, pages 4 (inset center), 11 (bottom), 12,
15 (right), 19 (top center), 19 (bottom), 22, 26, 28 (bottom), 31,
33 (top right), 34, 37 (top), 38 (bottom), 40 (inset), 41 (top center),
41 (bottom center), 41 (bottom right), 42 (left), 43 (inset)
Stephanie Siedman, Maui Nui Botanical Garden, Maui, Hawaii:
page 35
Wikipedia: pages 7 (row 1, left), 7 (row 3, left), 7 (row 3; right),
9 (bottom), 19 (bottom center), 21 (right)

Library and Archives Canada Cataloguing in Publication

Levine, Shar, 1953-
Plants : flowering plants, ferns, mosses, and other
plants / Shar Levine and Leslie Johnstone.

(A class of their own)
Includes index.
ISBN 978-0-7787-5376-6 (bound).--ISBN 978-0-7787-5390-2 (pbk.)

1. Plants--Classification--Juvenile literature.
2. Plants--Juvenile literature. I. Johnstone, Leslie
II. Title. III. Series: Class of their own

QK95.L49 2010   j580.1'2   C2009-907431-1

Library of Congress Cataloging-in-Publication Data

Levine, Shar, 1953-
Plants : flowering plants, ferns, mosses, and other plants / by Shar Levine and
Leslie Johnstone.
p. cm. -- (A class of their own)
Includes index.
ISBN 978-0-7787-5390-2 (pbk. : alk. paper) -- ISBN 978-0-7787-5376-6
(reinforced library binding : alk. paper)

1. Plants--Juvenile literature. I. Johnstone, Leslie. II. Title. III. Series.

QK49.L585 2010
580--dc22
                                                          2009051342

Crabtree Publishing Company

www.crabtreebooks.com   1-800-387-7650

Printed in the U.S.A./012010/BG20091216

Published in Canada
Crabtree Publishing
616 Welland Ave.
St. Catharines, Ontario
L2M 5V6

Published in the United States
Crabtree Publishing
PMB 59051
350 Fifth Avenue, 59th Floor
New York, New York 10118

Published in the United Kingdom
Crabtree Publishing
Maritime House
Basin Road North, Hove
BN41 1WR

Published in Australia
Crabtree Publishing
386 Mt. Alexander Rd.
Ascot Vale (Melbourne)
VIC 3032

Contents

WHAT ARE PLANTS?

The green grass between your toes, the shade of a red maple tree, and the crunchy apple you are about to eat—all are provided by plants. Plants do more than feed and shelter us. They also provide the material for our clothes and homes, the oxygen in the air we breathe, and medicines to make us healthy.

What Is a Plant?

Plants are organisms that use energy from sunlight to make food. They are made up of many cells working together for the benefit of the whole organism. Plant cells have cell walls, rigid structures containing fibers of cellulose, the material used to make the paper in this book.

CASE STUDY

Kingdom or Domain?

The way life-forms are grouped, or classified, is constantly changing. Traditionally, organisms were classified as either animal or plant. Over the years, many organisms have been grouped *alongside* animals and plants, rather than *within* those two groups. For years, the classification of living things has been based on six *kingdoms* of life—animals, plants, fungi, protists, bacteria, and archaea.

As scientists improve their understanding of the genetic makeup of living things, they can better compare organisms. This understanding has helped scientists figure out even more detailed groupings of living things. In the past, organisms were grouped according to their appearance. Appearances can be misleading, however. Two organisms may look similar, but their genetic makeup can be very different. For example, some yeasts might look like bacteria based on the fact that, like bacteria, they consist of a single round cell. Today, yeasts are known to be fungi, not bacteria.

Most scientists now believe that organisms should be classified using an even bigger grouping than kingdom. This level is called the *domain*. These scientists propose that life should be divided into three domains—Eukarya, Bacteria, and Archaea. Within the domain Eukarya are the four kingdoms of animals, plants, fungi, and protists. These kingdoms are more closely related to each other than to the domains of bacteria and archaea.

This is where things stand—for now. As scientists continue to make new discoveries, this system will undoubtedly turn out to be another chapter in the story of life!

EUKARYA

Protists
Plants
Animals
Fungi

BACTERIA

ARCHAEA

Most plants do not move once they are growing. Kingdom Plantae includes giant cedar trees, tiny mosses, beautiful roses, and spiny cacti. The fruits, vegetables, and grains we eat all come from plants.

Vascular and Non-Vascular Plants

Botanists, scientists who study plants, have divided plants into two large groups based on how water and nutrients travel within the plant. Vascular tissues are specialized groups of cells that form tubes to transport water and nutrients from the soil and the leaves to the rest of the plant. The simplest plants are the small, non-vascular plants, which don't have vascular tissues. Vascular plants have roots, stems, and leaves containing vascular tissues. These plants can have seeds and flowers, but non-vascular plants don't have seeds or flowers.

Non-vascular moss plants grow on bigleaf maple and Sitka spruce trees in the Hoh Rain Forest, Olympic National Park, in the state of Washington.

Sunflower seeds are a source of nutritious food for animals and humans.

Flower

Stem

Leaf

Seeds

From Domain to Species

Each individual type of plant is known as a species. No one knows for sure how many plant species are on the planet, but most estimates indicate more than 400,000. When scientists group plants together, they do this in levels, starting with domains, then kingdoms. Within a kingdom are several divisions. Each division consists of classes. Each class is made up of orders. Each order is made up of families. Each family contains genera (plural of *genus*). Each genus contains species. Several similar plants can be the same species but look quite different, so plant classification also often includes subspecies and cultivars, which are plants that have been specially bred for certain characteristics. For example, broccoli, cabbage, and Brussels sprouts are all different cultivars of the same species.

The name of a species is given using both the genus and the species name, so in the classification shown below, the scientific name for the Alberta wild rose is *Rosa acicularis*.

CLASSIFICATION OF THE ALBERTA WILD ROSE

Domain:	Eukarya	Organisms made up of complex cells
Kingdom:	Plantae	Plants
Division:	Magnoliophyta	Flowering plants
Class:	Magnoliopsida	Flowering plants with two seed leaves
Order:	Rosales	Related plants including ornamental and edible-fruit plants found in temperate regions including roses, elms, apples, and strawberries
Family:	Rosaceae	A group of herbs, shrubs, and trees that have five petals and a lot of stamens
Genus:	*Rosa*	Roses and wild roses
Species:	*acicularis*	Alberta wild rose

Plant Kingdom: Divisions

There are several different plant divisions, the category that comes just after the kingdom name (Plantae). There is no agreement on the exact number of divisions in the plant kingdom. Some sources give as few as four and others as many as 28. Some divisions, such as Pteridospermatophyta, only consist of extinct species. The plant divisions include the following:

Anthocerotophyta—Hornworts— non-vascular plants

Bryophyta—Mosses— non-vascular plants

Marchantiophyta—Liverworts— non-vascular plants

Lycopodiophyta—club mosses— vascular non-seed plants

Psilophyta—whisk ferns—vascular non-seed plants

Sphenophyta—horsetails—vascular non-seed plants

Polypodiophyta—ferns—vascular non-seed plants

Pinophyta—conifers—vascular seed plants

Cycadophyta—cycads—vascular seed plants

Ginkgophyta—Ginkgo plants— vascular seed plants

Magnoliophyta—flowering plants— vascular seed plants with flowers

Hornwort

Reindeer moss

Leafy liverwort

Fir club moss

Whisk fern

Horsetail cones

Tree ferns

Conifers

Sago cycad

Ginkgo leaves

Bleeding heart flowers

Plant Habitats

Scientists love to classify everything they study—and what better for them to classify than biomes of the world around them? Biomes are divisions of environments based on their living (biotic) and non-living (abiotic) parts. Non-living components are things like sunlight, soil, temperature, and moisture. The latitude, elevation, and climate are also considered abiotic factors. Living components include animals and plants but also fungi and bacteria.

Scientists describe between 11 and 16 different biomes. Basically, biomes are distinct geographical areas with particular conditions that allow specific plants and animals to thrive in these areas. For example, you wouldn't expect mosses to live in the Gobi desert, and you wouldn't expect to find a palm tree in Alaska. Neither of these plants would survive at the temperatures and humidity found in the new environment.

Here is a list of the major land biomes and some examples of the plant life found in them:

BIOMES	PLANTS
Tundra	Moss, low grasses, no trees
Boreal forest	Fir (coniferous trees), few ground plants
Temperate deciduous forest	Five layers of plants, trees, shrubs, berries, ferns, and mosses
Temperate rain forest	Very tall trees, mosses, ferns, berries
Grassland—tropical, temperate	Grasses, few trees
Tropical rain forest	Plants growing in abundance in layers, tall trees that stop sunlight from getting to the ground
Desert—hot and cold	Few if any plants
Permanent ice—polar ice	Moss, some flowers in Arctic

A musk ox female and calf eating low-growing plants on the Arctic tundra of Norway.

A misty, shaded tropical rain forest on the island of Borneo, Malaysia.

British Columbia—Coastal Temperate Rain Forest

CASE STUDY

The term *rain forest* makes most people think of the Amazon, but rain forests are also found in cooler regions. British Columbia, Canada, contains a coastal temperate rain forest. It has thick forests of tall trees, including pine, cedars, hemlocks, and Douglas firs. These trees are surrounded by moss, ferns, lichens, shrubs, berry bushes, and an abundance of wild flowers. The nutrient-rich environment is also home to a wide variety of animals including bears, deer, moose, and wolves. Both large and small birds make their nests in the old growth trees, and Pacific salmon are found in the streams.

In recent years, the mountain pine beetle has infested many of the pine trees, killing off vast sections of the forest and devastating the wildlife found there. The number of mountain pine beetles has increased because warmer winters have allowed greater numbers of the insects to survive.

Scientists collect insects in a Sitka spruce tree in a temperate rain forest.

INVASIVE SPECIES: A FANCY TERM FOR "WEED"

Taking a plant from where it is naturally found and transplanting it to another environment can have terrible consequences. The strawberry guava, Psidium cattleianum (left), was introduced to Hawaii about 50 years ago, probably from South America. It soon began taking over the forests, killing off the native plants. The roots of this tree form a thick, dense mat that stops native plants from thriving. This species has also been found to give off a chemical that poisons other plants growing near it.

THE BIOLOGY OF PLANTS

All plants have parts that function together to allow the plant to produce food, grow and develop, reproduce, and adjust to changes in their environment. With these parts, they are able to live successfully in all the different biomes of the world.

Making Their Own Food—Photosynthesis

Most plants are autotrophs, organisms that produce their own food. They have the process of photosynthesis, the ability to make their own food using sunlight and the simple chemicals carbon dioxide and water. Starting with these chemicals, plant cells form the sugar glucose and release oxygen gas into the atmosphere.

In plant cells, this process occurs in small, membrane-bound organelles called chloroplasts. Chloroplasts contain a green pigment called chlorophyll that the plants use to harness solar energy. The chlorophyll takes in, or absorbs, energy from the Sun, which is then used by the plant to make photosynthesis occur. Chloroplasts are found in any of the green parts of plants, but most are found in the leaves.

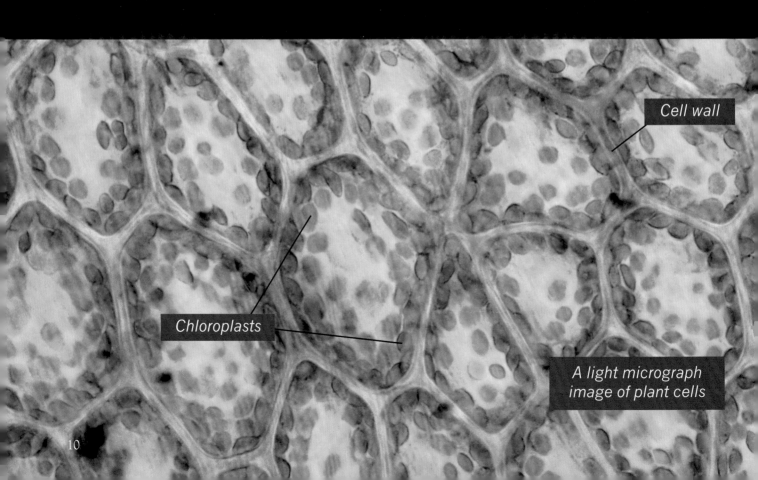

Cell wall

Chloroplasts

A light micrograph image of plant cells

Adaptations of the Leaf for Gas Exchange

Leaves have a flattened shape to increase the exposure of the plant cells to sunlight. They are usually only a few cells thick, so sunlight can enter all the cells. The outer surface of leaves and stems is covered by a waxy cuticle that keeps water from evaporating from the leaves. Leaves and stems get carbon dioxide from the air through adjustable pores called stomata (plural of *stoma*). The stomata open up during the day to allow carbon dioxide to enter and oxygen to exit. If a plant is in danger of drying out, the stomata close.

Protea leaves and flower

A GIFT OF LIFE FOR THE PLANET

Plants play an important role in the formation of our atmosphere. Most organisms, including plants, use oxygen in respiration and give off carbon dioxide gas. Plants also produce their own nutrition though photosynthesis, which causes them to give off oxygen gas. They give off more oxygen gas than they use, so if there were no plants, there would not be enough oxygen in the atmosphere to support life. The next time you take a breath, thank a plant!

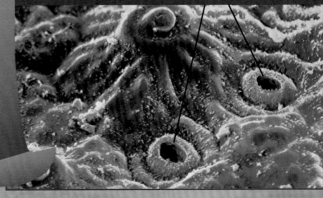

A scanning electron microscope image of stomata on the leaf of a protea plant.

PIGMENTS: MORE THAN JUST GREEN

Leaves can be different shades and colors depending on the amount of each pigment they contain. The green color of plants is produced by the pigment chlorophyll. When leaves turn color in the autumn, they lose the green chlorophyll, and the yellow and orange pigments, called carotenoids, and red pigments, called anthocyanins, are revealed. These pigments assist chlorophyll by absorbing some of the sunlight needed to harness energy from the Sun.

Simple and Compound Leaf Shapes

Leaves come in several different shapes, but they all share some structures in common. Most leaves have flattened parts called blades. The blades are attached to the plant's stem by a thin section called a petiole. Simple leaves have a single blade, which can be different shapes. Compound leaves have several blades, called leaflets, which are attached to the petiole.

Taking in Water and Minerals from the Soil

Plants need to take in water and minerals from their environments. Most plants have specialized tissues that transport water and minerals from the soil and carry the sugars produced by the plant from the leaves into the other plant tissues. These specialized tissues are found in roots and stems as well as in the veins of leaves in certain plants. The simplest plants, such as mosses, hornworts, and liverworts, lack these tissues, and water and minerals just enter the cells of these plants directly from their environments.

Leaves are the structures where most of the photosynthesis occurs. Leaves have veins made up of xylem and phloem.

The connecting structures between roots and leaves are the stems. Stems support the leaves and carry water and nutrients between the leaves and the roots.

Roots are the underground structures that anchor plants to the soil. They absorb water and nutrients from the soil and transport these materials upward to the stem. Vascular tissue called xylem is located in the center of the root.

Xylem and Phloem: The Stuff of Vascular Tissue

Plants first evolved to produce vascular tissues more than 400 million years ago. This allowed for the development of true roots, stems, and leaves, which are all plant parts containing vascular tissue.

Xylem and phloem are the two kinds of vascular tissue found in plants. Xylem conducts water and minerals up from the soil into the stem and leaves of the plant. It contains hollow cells with thick walls. These cells are joined together end to end to form a series of tubes. Phloem transports nutrients the plant has produced from one part of the plant to another through long, specialized cells.

This picture is a colored scanning electron micrograph (SEM) of a cross-section through a plant stem showing vascular tissue.

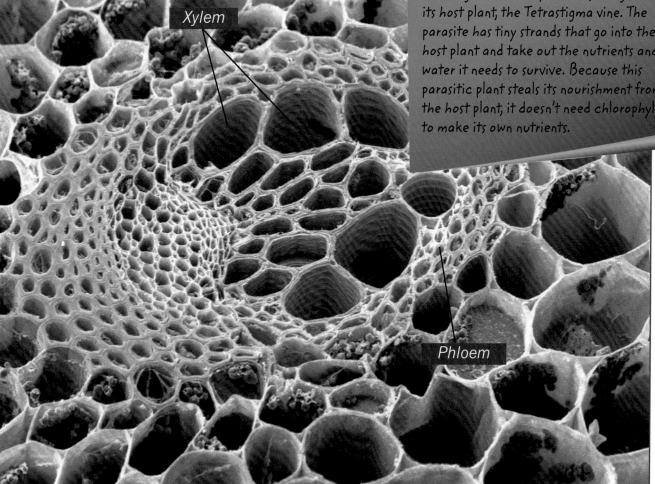

Xylem

Phloem

WHY MAKE MY OWN FOOD, WHEN I CAN EAT YOURS?

It's big. It's ugly. It stinks. Meet Rafflesia arnoldii (above), the largest flower in the world, measuring three feet (one meter) across and weighing over 24 pounds (11 kilograms). It is parasitic, living off its host plant, the Tetrastigma vine. The parasite has tiny strands that go into the host plant and take out the nutrients and water it needs to survive. Because this parasitic plant steals its nourishment from the host plant, it doesn't need chlorophyll to make its own nutrients.

**GIANT AMAZON
WATER LILY**

Kingdom: Plantae
Division: Magnoliophyta
Class: Magnoliopsida
Order: Nymphaeales
Family: Nymphaeaceae
Genus: *Victoria*
Species: *amazonica*

Giant Amazon Water Lily

CASE STUDY

The enormous Amazon water lily, the largest of all known water plants, boasts leaves that can be as wide as seven feet (two m). These record-setting leaves and the long stems that anchor the plant to the river bottom aren't the only fascinating features of these plants. Its flowers are amazing, as well. *Victoria amazonica* only blooms at night. On the first night, the flower (a female) is white and gives off a strong scent that attracts a species of beetle. At dawn, the flower closes, trapping the beetle inside. During the following day, the flower changes sexes and becomes a male. That night, the flower blooms again. This time it is bright pink. As the flower opens, it releases the beetle, which is covered with pollen. The beetle flies to another white lily, where the pollen rubs off onto the female, thus fertilizing the plant.

Rhizomes—ginger

Tubers—potatoes

Bulbs—onions

Corms–crocus flowers

STORAGE ORGANS

Glucose produced by plants is stored in the form of starch. Plants have developed several different types of storage organs that are modifications of the plant stems. These organs, including tubers, bulbs, corms, and rhizomes, store food until the plant needs it for growth. Many of these storage organs supply humans with food, as well!

Plants as Producers

Plants get their energy directly from sunlight. They are called producers because they produce food in the form of sugars and starches. Herbivores, or animals that eat plants, are called consumers. When they are eaten, these animals become energy sources for carnivores, which are animals that eat other animals. All animals that eat meat, including humans, actually rely on crops, such as wheat and corn, which are fed to the animals that provide their meat, as the initial source of their energy.

Finally, when animals and plants die, they are consumed by organisms, such as bacteria, that are called decomposers.

Plants Aren't Just for Food

In addition to being used for food, many plants contain chemicals that act as powerful medicines. Ethnobotany, the study of relationships between traditional societies and plants, includes an interest in how those societies use plants as medicines. The world's first enthnobiomedical forest reserve was created in Belize in 1993. Called the Terra Nova Rainforest Reserve, it is designed to ensure the protection of the plants the local healers use to treat people.

Local healers on the island of Samoa traditionally used the *Homalanthus nutans* (the common names of which include tropical bleeding heart and native poplar) to treat people suffering from yellow fever. They beat the stem, put it into hot water, and allowed it to steep. They then gave it to the patient. Scientists studied this plant and identified a substance called prostratin. Pharmaceutical companies are now producing this drug and are hoping to use it to treat people with HIV, the virus that causes AIDS.

Strawberry plants use vegetative reproduction. They throw out runners that take root and grow into new plants.

Parent plant

Runner

New plants

Reproduction

Plants can reproduce asexually and sexually. In asexual reproduction, the new plant is a clone, or identical copy, of its parent. A piece of plant can break off and grow into a new plant, or the plant can reproduce by vegetative reproduction. In this process, special cells in the stem or root of the plant form structures, such as bulbs, runners, or sprouts, that develop into a new plant.

When plants reproduce sexually, the new plant has the combined characteristics of each of the parent plants. All plants have a life cycle that includes what is called an alternation of generations. This means that there are two life stages: the gametophyte stage and the sporophyte stage.

The gametophyte grows from spores, tiny particles that include genetic information. In non-flowering plants such as mosses, liverworts, and hornworts, the leafy green gametophyte is quite prominent. This is the stage with which most people are familiar. In fruit trees, magnolias, and other flowering plants, the gametophyte is very small. The male gametophyte produces sperm, and the female gametophyte produces eggs—male and female reproductive cells. The sperm fertilize the eggs. The fertilized eggs develop to become the sporophytes, which are the mature plants that then release spores to begin the life cycle of a new generation of plants.

Annual, Biennial, and Perennial Plants

Among the higher vascular plants, there are three different life cycles. Annual plants live for only one year. They sprout in the spring, grow throughout the summer, form seeds in the fall, and then die. They are grown new from seed each year. Biennials have a two-year life cycle. They grow in the first year and form seeds and die in the second year. Perennial plants live for at least two years. Some of them may appear dead in the winter, but they re-grow their foliage in the spring from storage organs—such as rhizomes, bulbs, tubers, or corms—that are still part of the original plant and hold energy or water. They may also re-grow from roots, stems, or other parts of the plant that survive the winter in a dormant state—one in which their functions slow down.

Extinct In The Wild: *Brighamia insignis*

There are at least two ways of saving endangered plant species: in situ, protecting the plants where they grow; and ex situ, growing the plants in greenhouses or other preserves.

The *Brighamia insignis* (known as the Alula in Hawaiian) is considered extinct in the wild, but it grows in Hawaii in the gardens of the National Tropical Botanical Garden. This rare plant was first discovered by brave botanists who rappelled down sheer cliffs on the Na Pali coast of Kauai. They hand pollinated the plant and collected the seeds, which they then germinated. The plan is to reintroduce the plants into the wild once they develop. It might seem that a tropical paradise like Hawaii wouldn't have many threatened plant species, but about 40 percent of all the plants on the United States' endangered plants species list are found there.

BRIGHAMIA INSIGNIS (Alula)

Kingdom: Plantae
Division: Magnoliophyta
Class: Magnoliopsida
Order: Campanulales
Family: Campanulaceae
Genus: *Brighamia*
Species: *insignis*

CHAPTER TWO

NON-SEED PLANTS—
MOSSES, LIVERWORTS, AND HORNWORTS

Mosses, liverworts, and hornworts are non-seed plants. These plants produce tiny, hard reproductive cells called spores. They are the simplest types of plants. Their leaves and stems are non-vascular, so water and nutrients can only move through their cells directly from the environment. As a result, they tend to be quite small and live in damp habitats.

Mosses—Division Bryophyta

Mosses grow together to form a dense carpet containing hundreds of plants. Each individual plant has simple leaves arranged in a spiral around the stem. This green leafy structure does not have vascular tissue, but it may contain a few cells in the stem that water can pass through. The stem is anchored to the ground by a colorless group of cells.

Mosses will take advantage of a wide range of places to grow—if the conditions are right!

Moss

Mosses can grow in a wide variety of habitats, as long as there is enough moisture so the plants do not dry out. They can grow on poor and rocky soil that would not support other plants. After an event such as a forest fire has removed plant material from a region, mosses are usually among the first plants to grow in the barren area. These and other early returning plants are called Pioneer species. The anchoring of mosses can help prevent erosion by keeping soil on rocky hillsides.

Liverworts—Division Marchantiophyta

Liverworts have many similarities to mosses. In fact, they used to be included in the same division. Some species of liverworts have leafy stems like those of the mosses. Other species have a flattened broad body called a thallus. The thallus is thought to resemble a liver in appearance— hence *liverwort* as a collective name for these plants.

Liverwort

Hornworts—Division Anthocerotophyta

At first glance, a hornwort may look just like a liverwort. They are similar in structure, but there are a few differences related to the structure of their reproductive parts. Just like liverworts, hornworts live in areas that are continuously kept damp.

Hornwort

The leaves are in a spiral around the stem.

A close-up view of moss

The plant is held in the ground by a few colorless cells, but no roots.

Moss plants

Leafy green
gametophytes

Sporophyte

Life Cycle with Alternation of Generations

All plants have a life cycle that includes what is called an alternation of generations. What this means is that there are two life stages: the gametophyte stage and the sporophyte stage.

In mosses, liverworts, and hornworts, the leafy green gametophyte grows from spores. The gametophyte produces sperm and eggs, which are the male and female reproductive cells. The sperm must swim through water to fertilize the eggs, which is one of the reasons these plants live in damp places. The fertilized egg develops to become the sporophyte, which then matures and releases spores.

Mosses and liverworts have sporophytes that grow at the top of the gametophyte plant. They look like tiny brownish capsules suspended on the end of long stalks. When the spores ripen, the capsule bursts and the spores are shed.

Moss Habitats

Mosses and their relatives can live anywhere there is a lot of water. They are abundant in wetlands such as swamps and bogs. They are also found in the world's rain forests or along the banks of streams. Many species can tolerate cold temperatures and poor soil conditions that would prevent the growth of other plants. Mosses are the most abundant plants found in tundra, the treeless regions in the far north.

Bog Fires: One Way of Saving a Habitat

Bogs are wetlands covered with a thick layer of mosses growing on a mat of dead vegetation. Bogs are beneficial for the environment in several ways. They store and filter water. They are also perfect habitats for mosses.

It may seem strange, but bogs, as wet as they may be, can catch on fire! While forest fires can be very destructive, a bog fire can be a good thing for nature. Here's how it works. Over time, trees begin to take over sections of a bog and start to turn it into a forest. A fire will burn down these trees and return the wetlands to conditions that are better to maintain the bog. With fewer trees and more mosses growing, the bog will be healthier. As long as the bog has plenty of water, it can return to its previous state after a fire.

SPHAGNUM MOSS

Sphagnum is a genus of mosses that thrive in bogs. These mosses act as a natural sponge, absorbing more than their own weight in water. Over time, as fresh layers of moss grow on top of dead moss plants, the compacted material becomes peat. Peat moss has been used as a fuel and also by gardeners as a way of keeping moisture in the soil. Environmentalists are concerned that widespread use of peat moss for gardening may be destroying the bog environment. The image above shows peat being dug out of the ground in blocks.

THE STAR MOSS

The star moss (Tortula ruralis) is very unusual. It lives in the desert and can completely dry out without dying. Generally, when a moss dries out it cannot come back to life. When the Star Moss gets wet, however, it immediately returns to a more common moss texture and shape. Within hours, the moss returns to a green color.

FERNS AND THEIR RELATIVES—
SEEDLESS VASCULAR PLANTS

Ferns, horsetails, and club mosses produce spores, but no seeds. They are the first plants to have developed a vascular system of cells arranged to form pathways for water and nutrients.

Bigger Than Non-Vascular Plants

The development of a vascular system allows these plants to be much larger than the simpler mosses and other non-vascular plants. As we have just learned, mosses tend to be quite small and are non-vascular, and they are therefore found living close to the damp places in the ground where they can absorb water and nutrients directly. In contrast, species of tree ferns can be over 80 feet (24 m) high. Another feature of these plants that makes them different from the mosses is that the part of the plant that is most visible is not the gametophyte, but the sporophyte.

It's Not Easy Being Seedless

Ferns and other seedless vascular plants can grow in a wide variety of habitats, including moist, shady forests, damp bogs, deserts, and high up on mountainsides. Seedless vascular plants need moisture to reproduce, as their sperm cells must travel through a film of water to reach their eggs. As a result, these plants tend to grow in areas that are damp for at least part of the year. Most grow in the soil, but some can grow out of the sides of trees. They often inhabit areas where flowering plants will not grow successfully. Some species of these plants are prized for use in gardens, while other species are considered weeds.

Fiddlehead fern frond

Whisk Ferns—Division Psilophyta

Whisk ferns closely resemble the first vascular plants that evolved more than 400 million years ago. They have stems that are mostly below ground, but they do not have true roots or leaves. The stems are anchored with a group of cells, similar to those found in mosses.

Club Mosses—Division Lycopodiophyta

Club moss

Club mosses are not actually mosses. Unlike mosses, they have true roots, leaves, and stems. Their leaves are small and narrow with a single vein of vascular tissue that runs up the center of the leaf. They have stems that can be upright, or they can run along the ground. Many of the club mosses grow on other plants, but they are not parasites, as they do not harm the host plant. Some club moss species are used by florists for greenery and by gardeners as a ground cover. Modern club mosses are small plants, but ancient club mosses grew as large as trees and formed the first forests.

Horsetails—Division Sphenophyta

Horsetails are different from club mosses because they have tall, hollow, green-jointed stems and a separate cone. The surface of the brownish cone is covered with tiny star-shaped structures that contain the spores of the plant. The round stem has segments surrounded by rough green branches poking out from the joint. Although these plants are found around the world, there are only about 30 different species. The plant is very ancient, having been around for about 300 million years.

Spore cone

Horsetail branch

GREEN SCOURING PADS

Scrubbing dirty dishes usually requires a rough scouring pad. In a pinch, a horsetail branch makes a useful and environmentally safe alternative to a store-bought brush. The plant contains small fibers of silica, the chemical found in glass, that comes in handy for removing food from pots, polishing some kinds of metals, and even sanding wooden surfaces.

Ferns—Division Polypodiophyta

The most numerous group of seedless vascular plants are ferns. Ferns have true vascular tissues with strong roots and either creeping or underground stems. Their characteristic large leaves, called fronds, emerge from the ground coiled up and looking like the handle of a violin. These curled fronds are called fiddleheads and are sought after by gourmet diners as a tasty delicacy. Ferns live in areas with little light, such as the forest floor. They grow best in areas that are damp for all or part of the year because they need water to reproduce.

Fern Life Cycle

This mature sporophyte has clusters of sporangia, called sori (brown dots shown here), on the underside of its fronds.

Mature ferns

The sporangia (black) release microscopic spores.

A light micrograph of young fern

A new sporophyte grows from the zygote.

A spore grows into a young gametophyte.

The sperm fertilizes the egg here to form a zygote.

Chinese Ladder Brake Fern

Look around for a fern, and you will usually find one growing in the shade. Unlike just about every other fern, however, the Chinese Ladder Brake (*Pteris vittata*) loves growing in sunlight. It also doesn't mind chemicals that would normally kill plants and people alike. Scientists in Florida have grown these ferns on soil that contains arsenic, a very toxic substance. They found that the plant began to absorb or draw in the chemicals from the contaminated ground. Even stranger, the more arsenic the plant had, the bigger it grew. Researchers are interested in this plant's abilities to take in arsenic as it is a natural way of ridding the environment of a dangerous substance.

CHINESE LADDER BRAKE

Kingdom: Plantae
Division: Polypodiophyta
Class: Polypodiopsida
Order: Polypodiales
Family: Pteridaceae
Genus: *Pteris*
Species: *Pteris vittata*

CHAPTER FOUR

GYMNOSPERMS—
CONIFERS, CYCADS, AND GINKGOES

One hundred million years ago, Earth's forests were filled with gymnosperms, the non-flowering seed plants. Many of these early plant species are now extinct. The word gymnosperm means "naked seed." These were the first plants with seeds. Unlike the seeds of the flowering plants, these seeds are not enclosed in fruit.

What Is a Seed?

Plants that only produce spores, such as mosses and ferns, need water to reproduce. The evolution of seeds allowed plants to reproduce without open water. Seeds are tiny plants encased in a protective coating with a supply of nutrients. The tiny plants are called embryos, and if the seed is placed in an environment where the plant can grow, it will grow to become an adult plant. Once a seed is planted, it begins the process of germination, or growth, to become the adult plant.

Conifers—Division Pinophyta

Conifers, such as pines, firs, cedar, and hemlock, are the dominant trees in cold, dry biomes, such as the northern boreal forest. They have adapted to colder climates and the scarcity of water in several ways.

Modern gymnosperms include rare plants such as the cycads and ginkgoes, as well as the more abundant conifers.

These trees have green leaves that most species keep all year round. This allows them to produce food and grow slowly for most of the year. The leaves are small needles or scales with a thick, waterproof cuticle, so water loss from the leaves is kept to a minimum. This is especially beneficial during cold winters, when water is frozen and plants experience conditions that are similar to a drought.

Many species of conifers grow as cone-shaped trees. This shape allows them to shed snow in the winter without breaking branches. Finally, the sap of conifers can contain chemicals called resins that act as a kind of anti-freeze, keeping nutrients and water moving through the plant in cold weather.

Reproduction—Alternation of Generations in Conifers

Conifers reproduce using structures called cones. These cones contain the gametophytes and are grown on the male and female sporophyte plants. The male, or pollen, cone produces pollen, which is the male gametophyte. Pollen grains are tiny particles, and clouds of them are released by the male cone. Carried by the wind, they travel to the female, or seed, cones. The female cone has woody scales that are arranged in a spiral. Each scale has two ovules, or immature eggs, attached at its base. These develop into the egg cells. When the pollen grain lands on the scale, it grows a tube that links the male and female gametophytes, and fertilization occurs. The fertilized egg begins to develop and becomes a seed. When the cone ripens, it releases its seeds. If the seed lands on fertile soil, it germinates and a new tree grows.

Male, or pollen, cones releasing pollen into the wind

Female seed cone

Cone after releasing seeds

Pine seeds shelled and unshelled

Wood

Wood is the xylem tissue from the stem of the tree. Conifers produce softwood. Hardwood comes from flowering trees, such as oak. Some softwood is relatively hard, and some hardwood is relatively soft, so the names don't always reflect the true strength of the wood.

Each year, trees grow new woody layers between the existing wood and the bark, or outer coating of the tree. If the tree is cut across the stem, these layers appear as rings. These "growth rings" are used to determine the age of the tree. The rings' sizes give scientists information about growing conditions, such as levels of precipitation during the tree's growth.

Growth rings

Ginkgo Biloba—Division Ginkgophyta

The Ginkgo is like an only child. It is the only plant in its division, with no other living relatives. Scientists consider this tree to be a living fossil, which is a term used to describe a species that hasn't changed at all during its very long life. Until recently, it was thought to be extinct in the wild. The leaves have an unusual fan shape, with a slit down the middle and parallel veins. The trees are either male or female, and the female produces something that looks like a fruit, but isn't. A soft, smelly shell or coat covers a seed. Despite its similar appearance to an apricot, this shell is not good for eating. The seed inside this shell is edible and considered a delicacy in Japan.

Ginkgo tree

Ginkgo leaves have traditionally been used as the basis for a number of herbal medicines.

28

Cycads—Division Cycadophyta

The cycads, like the ginkgoes, were abundant millions of years ago. Modern cycads consist of about 300 species that grow in tropical or subtropical regions. These slow-growing plants look like large ferns or palm trees, but they are not related to either ferns or palms. Almost half of all cycad species are endangered or threatened due to destruction of their habitats and harvesting.

KING SAGO PALM

Kingdom:	Plantae
Division:	Cycadophyta
Class:	Cycadopsida
Order:	Cycadales
Family:	Cycadaceae
Genus:	*Cycas*
Species:	*revoluta*

CASE STUDY

King Sago Palm

Names can be deceiving. The king sago palm is not a palm—and obviously, it is not a king. It is a member of the Cycad family, and what makes it interesting is that it is one of the oldest of the seed-bearing plants. Fossil remains of this plant show that it grew on Earth 34–55 million years ago. Although the plant originated in Asia, it can now be found in greenhouses and gardens around the world. The plants are either male or female. The male produces a tall cone, while the female plant has a round, feathery cone. When germinated, the plant has large seeds with red skin. The seeds are very poisonous, and if they are eaten they will sicken people and can easily kill a dog or even larger mammals.

Welwitschia mirabilis

What has two leaves, grows in the desert, can survive on less than one inch (25 millimeters) of rain, and lives for more than a thousand years? Meet the *Welwitschia mirabilis*, a very bizarre plant that is only found in the wild in the Namib Desert in Africa. Unlike other plants that shed their leaves and grow new ones, this plant keeps its original two leaves over its entire life. During that time, the leaves may split and take on long, twisted shapes. The plant itself looks as if it was run over with a steamroller. Older specimens have wide bases that can be over 30 feet (9.1 m) in circumference, with roots that reach down 100 feet (30 m) into the ground.

Welwitschia mirabilis belongs to the division Gnetophyta, which includes about 70 species of plants. Gnetophytes can be shrubs, vines, or small trees.

CHAPTER FIVE

ANGIOSPERMS— FLOWERING PLANTS

Angiosperms, or flowering plants, have been the most successful plant group for the past 100 million years. There are more than 400,000 different species of these plants. Flowering plants provide us with nearly all our food. Orchids, peas, and apple trees are all angiosperms. So are grasses, roses, and buttercups.

It Pays to Advertise!

This group of plants has flowers, fruits, and seeds enclosed in a shell-like covering. These are all adaptations that have helped the spread of angiosperms.

Flowers are the plant's way of advertising that lovely pollen and nectar are to be found within. It is their purpose to attract animals that can carry pollen from one plant to another. Certain flowers are so closely tied to the insects that pollinate them that if the insects die out, so do the flowers.

Some angiosperms also release large numbers of pollen grains to the wind.

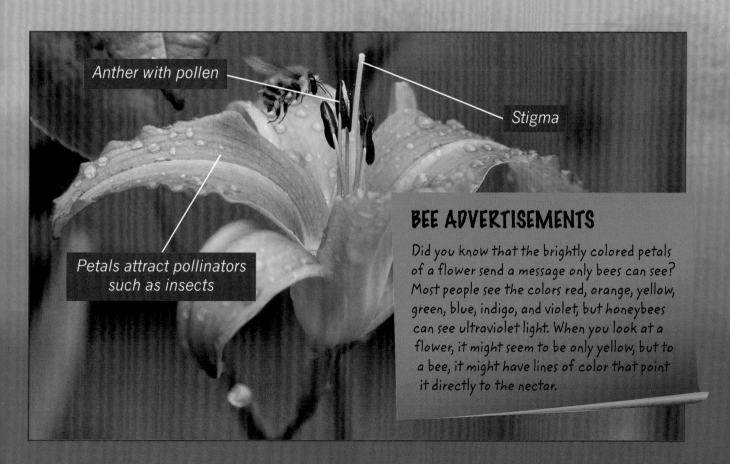

Anther with pollen

Stigma

Petals attract pollinators such as insects

BEE ADVERTISEMENTS

Did you know that the brightly colored petals of a flower send a message only bees can see? Most people see the colors red, orange, yellow, green, blue, indigo, and violet, but honeybees can see ultraviolet light. When you look at a flower, it might seem to be only yellow, but to a bee, it might have lines of color that point it directly to the nectar.

Life Cycle of the Angiosperm

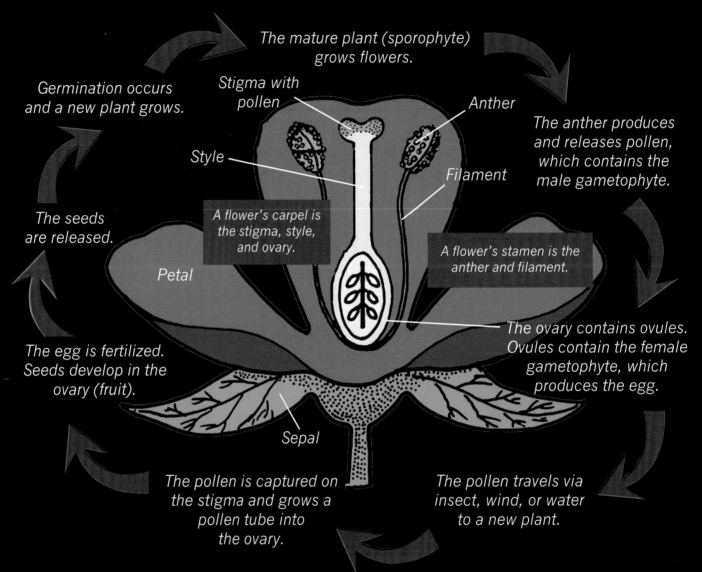

The mature plant (sporophyte) grows flowers.

Germination occurs and a new plant grows.

Stigma with pollen

Anther

The anther produces and releases pollen, which contains the male gametophyte.

Style

Filament

The seeds are released.

A flower's carpel is the stigma, style, and ovary.

A flower's stamen is the anther and filament.

Petal

The egg is fertilized. Seeds develop in the ovary (fruit).

The ovary contains ovules. Ovules contain the female gametophyte, which produces the egg.

Sepal

The pollen is captured on the stigma and grows a pollen tube into the ovary.

The pollen travels via insect, wind, or water to a new plant.

Fruits

Fruits are a plant's way of making sure that seeds travel over greater distances than if the seeds just fell straight to the ground. The ovary surrounding the seeds becomes a fruit. An animal eats the fruit. The seeds go through the animal's digestive system and are deposited along with a mass of nutrient-rich organic material (the animal's feces) in a new location where the seed can then grow.

Some fruits, such as burrs, are dispersed not by being eaten but by sticking to the fur of passing animals. Other fruits, such as those of dandelions, act as tiny parachutes allowing the wind to better disperse the seeds.

Fruits are the ripened ovary of the flower containing the seeds. Many foods that you might think are not a fruit actually are fruits. Pumpkins, eggplants, tomatoes, and peas are all fruits, even though they aren't sweet. Rhubarb can be used to make pies, but it is a stem, not a fruit.

Animals eat fruit and spread seeds in their feces.

Burrs attach to animals.

Some seeds disperse in the wind.

Broad Leaves

Plants use their leaves to absorb sunlight. Broad leaves have a larger surface than needles, so they can absorb more sunlight. Leaves can easily dry out, so plants have adapted to the conditions where they grow. In areas with plentiful water, plants can grow broad leaves without as much danger of the leaves drying out. In drier areas, the plants can have waxy cuticles to prevent water loss. In colder regions with less sunlight, broad leaf plants can lose their leaves in winter to prevent the loss of water from the plant at a time when it would not receive much sunlight.

One disadvantage of broad leaves is that they are a more appealing food for animals than are smaller leaves such as pine needles. As a result, flowering plants have evolved to provide themselves with various forms of protection. Thorns, spines, and nasty-tasting resins all protect these plants from becoming dinner. Certain plants have developed unpleasant-tasting or even poisonous chemicals. These chemicals may taste bad to animals searching for plants to eat, but they provide us with caffeine and medicines such as aspirin and codeine, as well as spices such as pepper, mustard, and vanilla.

SEED BANKS

There is a Global Seed Vault, located deep inside a frozen mountain in Norway. It contains over 90,000 food crop seed samples from places around the world. In the event of a terrible natural disaster, the world would still have seeds to begin planting food again. Another seed bank located in Britain is dedicated to saving the seeds of wild plants.

A new shoot grows alongside a protective thorn.

Cultivated Plants—Take a Walk on the Wild Side

Plants grown in the wild can be very different from those carefully bred and cultivated by growers over many generations. Growers choose individual plants with desirable characteristics and deliberately breed them to get a plant that does what they want. Bananas are a good example of the results of this practice. Wild varieties are smaller than those found in grocery stores, and they contain large seeds from which the plant can be grown. Growers breed and crossbreed different varieties of the plant to produce the plantains and sweet bananas found in the supermarket today.

Commercially cultivated pepper plants

Cultivated bananas, those bred by farmers, are sterile. This means that they have no seeds and the plant could no longer exist without human intervention. Modern banana plants must be grown from shoots or tissues from growing plants, which are then transplanted into soil. Because plants are normally conserved by seeds, scientists are concerned that if a new disease strikes cultivated bananas, it might wipe out the gene pool.

Dicots and Monocots

Flowering plants have traditionally been divided into two main classes—Magnoliopsida, or dicots, and Liliopsida, or monocots. This classification is changing due to new evidence from genetic studies involving these plants and will probably continue to change for some time as scientists learn more. More than one in four flowering plant species are monocots, and the rest can be grouped with the dicots.

MONOCOTS	DICOTS
Have a single cotyledon or seed leaf that forms in the embryo	Have two cotyledons
Leaves have parallel veins	Leaves have net-like veins
Xylem and phloem tissues in stem are arranged in a ring	Xylem and phloem scattered throughout

THE PREGNANT BANANA

Kingdom: Plantae
Division: Magnoliophyta
Class: Liliopsida
Order: Zingiberales
Family: Musaceae
Genus: *Musa*
Species: *paradisiaca*

CASE STUDY

The Pregnant Banana: *Musa paradisiaca*

The strangest banana in the world is the Mai'a Hapai. Unlike other banana trees, where the fruit hangs down and is easy to pick, this one sometimes fruits inside the core of its trunk, giving the banana plant the appearance of being pregnant. Growers know when the fruit is ripe by watching the number of ants crawling on the trunk. When there are a lot of ants, the fruit inside is ripe. A sharp knife is used to cut open the trunk and release the small bananas that are attached to a fruit stalk that looks just like an umbilical cord.

FRANKEN FRUIT

In 2006, six percent of the genetically modified (GM) crops in the world were grown in Canada. GM crops have had their genetic material changed by scientists. Many of these crops were transgenic. This means that the plants contained genetic material from two different species. For example, a gene could be transplanted from a tomato into an apple to keep the apple from spoiling. Most of the GM crops currently grown are designed to be insect, weather, or herbicide resistant. Scientists are developing plants that may be able to produce plastics or vaccines. Some of this research is controversial, as the risks associated with changing the genetics of a plant or an animal are not completely understood.

CHAPTER SIX

BUTTERCUPS, ROSES, AND OTHER DICOTS

The majority of the flowering plants are found in the Magnoliopsida, or dicot, group. Dicots are a very diverse group of plants, ranging from enormous trees to tiny flowers. They can be small herbs, woody shrubs, climbing vines, tall trees, prickly berries, and spiny cacti.

What Is a Tree?

Some of the oldest living plants on our planet are trees. Trees can be members of many different orders and families. They are tall perennial plants with a single stem, called a trunk. They have branches with leaves that are supported by the trunk and that can provide shelter for smaller plants and animals. Tree trunks are made of woody material, and wood cut from trees is an important building material and fuel used to cook food and heat homes. Tree roots anchor soil in the areas where they grow to prevent erosion.

Shrubs are not trees, either because they have multiple stems or they never grow to be as tall.

Too Many to Name Them All

Many of the foods we eat, and even some of the clothes we wear, come from these flowering plants. There are too many species to mention them all, but here are a few examples of some of the more interesting dicot families.

THE RANUNCULACEAE OR BUTTERCUP FAMILY

Most of the members of the buttercup family (shown right) are small herbs, shrubs, or vines with divided leaves. This family includes cultivated flowers such as clematis and anemones, as well as weeds like the buttercup. All species of buttercups are poisonous when eaten by horses and cattle. The bad taste of the plants and the mouth blisters they cause usually mean they don't get eaten. When fields are over-grazed and the animals are really hungry, grazers are occasionally poisoned by the lovely-looking buttercup.

THE CACTACEAE OR CACTUS FAMILY

Members of the cactus family are ideally adapted for living in a dry environment. They have tiny leaves, thick skin, and a waxy cuticle or covering to retain water. These plants tend to grow in a barrel or sphere shape to reduce the surface of the plant, another adaptation for reducing water loss. Tiny spines serve two purposes: they protect the plant from being eaten; and they help shade the plant from the Sun's rays. The roots of cacti are usually shallow and spread outward over a large area to allow the plant to collect water from infrequent rains.

THE MAGNOLIACEAE OR MAGNOLIA FAMILY

The impressive magnolia tree can grow to a height of 100 feet (30 m) or more. Its large, stiff evergreen leaves and showy white blossoms make it a favorite of gardeners in warmer climates. The flowers, which have six or more petals, are thick, so they aren't damaged by the beetles that crawl inside to pollinate them. Most of the species in this family are trees or large shrubs.

The fruit of certain kinds of prickly pear cacti (Opuntia ficus-indica) is a delicacy eaten in the southern United States, Mexico, the Middle East, and other lands around the Mediterranean Sea. Once the outer skin is peeled to remove the tiny spikes, the flesh inside is sweet and tasty.

Naming Things

Who gets to name new species? Whoever discovers a new species gets to name it. Scientists with a sense of humor sometimes name their new species after famous people, and as long as they follow the international rules for taxonomy, they can have fun.

Many plants are named after the people who discover them or in honor of famous botanists. Numerous people have had roses named for them. Roses with famous people's names in them include three different roses named in honor of Britain's Queen Elizabeth II and others named after explorers such as Amelia Earhart, presidents such as John F. Kennedy, or actresses such as Audrey Hepburn, Elizabeth Taylor, and Julie Andrews.

THE SALICACEAE OR WILLOW FAMILY

Willows and poplars are members of this family of trees. They grow abundantly in the temperate regions of the northern hemisphere. Willow bark contains salicylic acid, which was a popular folk treatment for pain and fever and can be used to make aspirin and remedies for pain, diarrhea, nausea, and other intestinal problems. Look for willows near bodies of water. Both the graceful tree willows (above) and the decorative pussy willows are members of this family.

THE MALVACEAE OR MALLOW FAMILY

What does your chocolate bar have in common with your cotton socks? They are both made from plants in the mallow family. The seeds of cacao (which grow inside the pods seen above) are used to make chocolate, and the fuzz on the seeds of the cotton plant are used to make cotton thread. The herbs, shrubs, and trees in this family have lobed leaves with veins that spread outward like the fingers on a hand.

THE ROSACEAE OR ROSE FAMILY

The rose family includes the roses (above), as you would imagine, and it also contains many of the more popular kinds of fruits and nuts such as peaches, apples, almonds, and cherries. The trees, shrubs, and herbs in this family have either fruit that surrounds the seeds or fruit with the seeds on the outside, such as strawberries.

Carnivorous Plants

Plants that live in habitats with poor soil that provide very few nutrients sometimes rely on other forms of food—such as animals. Carnivorous, or flesh-eating, plants come in a variety of shapes and sizes, all designed for one purpose—to trap their meals. While there are many different species of carnivorous or insectivorous plants, there are several ways they capture their prey. Some have leaves that act like traps, closing when an insect lands on them, or catching them in a maze. Others have sticky, glue-like surfaces on their leaves. Once the insect is caught, the plant digests it and extracts the minerals and nutrients it needs to survive.

CASE STUDY

Attenborough's Pitcher Plant (*Nepenthes attenboroughii*)

In 2009, scientists made a startling discovery. In a remote and inaccessible mountainous area of the Philippines, they found one of the world's largest pitcher plants. They named the plant after Sir David Attenborough, a famous British TV star noted for his work on nature shows. The plant has a mouth large enough to capture giant centipedes and huge spiders. Theoretically, it could kill and digest a small rodent, should one be careless enough to fall in. The edge of the mouth has sweet nectar that attracts prey. The inside surface of the pitcher is slippery, so once the animal falls in, it cannot climb out. Soon, the special liquids inside the pitcher begin to break down and digest the animal.

NEPENTHES ATTENBOROUGHII	
Kingdom:	Plantae
Division:	Magnoliophyta
Class:	Magnoliopsida
Order:	Caryophyllales
Family:	Nepenthaceae
Genus:	*Nepenthes*
Species:	*attenboroughii*

CHAPTER SEVEN

LILIES, ORCHIDS, AND OTHER MONOCOTS

Lilies, orchids, and other monocots are members of the class Liliopsida. These plants have a single seed leaf and leaves with parallel veins. There are several families of monocots, including lilies, grasses, irises, and orchids. In addition to these families, smaller families such as the Zingiberaceae or ginger family, the Arecaceae or palm family, and the Musaceae or banana family belong to this class.

The Liliaceae or Lily Family

Lilies are mostly beautiful showy flowers, such as tulips, hyacinths, and day lilies. The flowers have their petals and sepals separated into six parts. They have six stamens (male parts) and one carpel (female part). They can have fruits that are typically capsules or berries.

Most lilies are herbs, but a few, such as the Joshua tree, are woody perennials. There are two genera of lilies that are grown for food: allium, which includes onions and garlic; and asparagus.

Aloes are also lilies. The leaves, pulp, juice, and roots of these plants are used for medicinal purposes. Aloe juice can be used to reduce the pain of a mild sunburn.

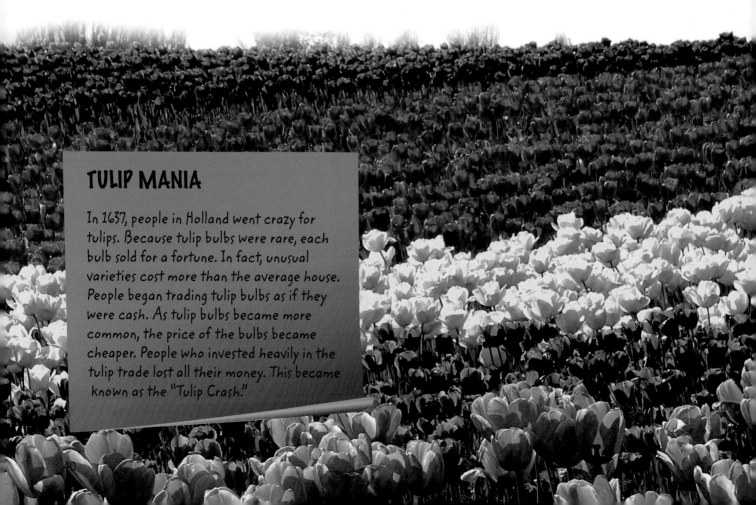

TULIP MANIA

In 1637, people in Holland went crazy for tulips. Because tulip bulbs were rare, each bulb sold for a fortune. In fact, unusual varieties cost more than the average house. People began trading tulip bulbs as if they were cash. As tulip bulbs became more common, the price of the bulbs became cheaper. People who invested heavily in the tulip trade lost all their money. This became known as the "Tulip Crash."

40

The Gramineae or Grass Family

Grasses have supplied mammals with food since the days before recorded history. The fruit of grasses is usually a grain. People and animals in the Mediterranean region ate wheat, rye, barley, and oats. In the Americas, the Aztecs and Mayans ate corn, and in Asia, the diet consisted of rice and millet. Whether as grass, grains, or cereals, grasses continue to provide humans and animals with food. They are the dominant plant in grasslands, supporting millions of grazing animals.

These plants have small flowers and leaves with long, linear blades. The leaves are the key feature of grasses; they grow from the leaf base, so if the blade is cut it grows back. This allows animals to keep eating the same blade of grass over and over again. This is why people have to keep mowing their lawns all summer long.

Bamboos are the largest grasses. These evergreen strong perennials are used for construction in some parts of the world and as decoration in gardens. Plants that resemble bamboo are the sugar canes. Sugar-producing species of grasses are found in the tropical biomes. Cane is cut, then processed and used to make sugar, molasses, and rum.

Lawns are made from sod-producing grasses. These perennials cover large areas of the earth, in meadows and around people's homes.

Joshua tree

Aloe plant

Bamboo used for construction scaffolding

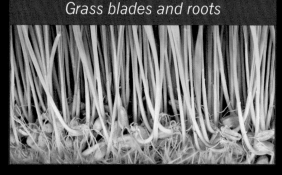
Grass blades and roots

COCO DE MER

The Coco de Mer palm has the largest fruit of any plant. This gigantic fruit contains one to four seeds and is called the "butt nut" for its resemblance to a part of human anatomy!

The Iridaceae or Iris Family

Like lilies, irises are a family of plants with large showy flowers, including irises, gladioli, freesia, and crocuses. The flowers of the members of the iris family are similar to those of lilies, although many have three large petals. The position of the ovary in lilies is within the flower at the base of the petals, while in irises the ovary is below the level where the petals attach. These perennial herbs grow from rhizomes, bulbs, or corms and have leaves and stalks that last for only one season, then die down in the winter and re-grow the next year.

The shape of the iris flower is ideally suited for the insects that pollinate it. The large petals give the insect a place to land. As an insect forages for nectar, it comes in contact with the stigma first and can deposit any pollen from another iris that it is carrying. On the way back out of the flower, the insect picks up new pollen from the anther. This pollen can be carried onto the next plant.

An iris flower

The Orchidaceae or Orchid Family

Orchids are the largest family of flowering plants, and the list of orchids is growing by about 800 new species every year. These plants can grow in soil, on trees, and even on dead and decaying plants. Most orchids are found in tropical regions, and a few species grow wild in temperate biomes. They are perennial with leaves that often stay green for several years. The plants grow from tubers, bulbs, or thickened roots.

Orchid flowers are highly adapted for insect pollination. Their sepals and petals act as a stage to attract and support pollinating insects. The stamens and carpels are fused together, and pollen hangs in masses called pollinia. Insects lift the pollinia and place them on the stigma so the pollen can enter and fertilize the egg. Some orchids self pollinate. Orchid growers try to reproduce the insect's role by using small paintbrushes to transfer pollen from one plant to another.

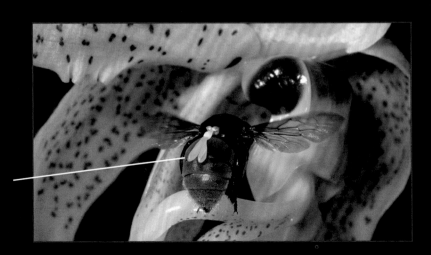

A bee with bright yellow pollinia on its back visiting an orchid flower

VANILLA ORCHID

Kingdom: Plantae
Division: Magnoliophyta
Class: Liliopsida
Order: Asparagales
Family: Orchidaceae
Genus: *Vanilla*
Species: *planifolia*

CASE STUDY

Vanilla planifolia: Orchids and Ice Cream

Orchids come in many shapes and sizes. They can be snowy white, deep purple, or canary yellow. But did you know they can also be tasty? The vanilla that flavors ice cream, cakes, or even drinks comes from *Vanilla planifolia*, one of the many species of the vanilla orchid. The long pods are the fruits of the plant, and they are picked, cured, and processed. Because of its long, brown shape, the pod is frequently misnamed "the bean."

To make vanilla flavoring, a pod can be scraped and placed in alcohol. Vanilla extract is an artificial flavoring made from a byproduct of paper and pulp processing and contains no natural "vanilla."

An opened vanilla pod

Glossary

angiosperms Flowering plants

annual Living for one year or less

anthocyanin Red or blue pigment found in flowers and plants

asexual reproduction Reproduction in which an organism produces smaller copies of itself without combining with another organism

autotrophs Organisms that make their own food by photosynthesis

biennial Living for two years

biomes Divisions of environments based on their biotic and abiotic parts; distinctive communities of plants and animals adapted to the prevailing conditions

biotic Having to do with living parts of the environment

blade The flat section of the leaf of a plant

carnivorous Feeding on animals

carotenoids Red or yellow pigment found in flowers and plants

cell The smallest structural or functioning unit of an organism, usually, but not always, consisting of cytoplasm, or protoplasm, and a nucleus surrounded by a membrane

chlorophyll Green pigment found in plants used in photosynthesis

chloroplasts Tiny membrane-bound structures containing chlorophyll and found in plant cells

classification The method scientists use to name and organize organisms into groups

conifer A tree that has cones and needle-like or scale-like leaves

corm An underground storage organ found in some plants consisting of a rounded, swollen stem base

cultivate To raise or grow for a specific purpose or to develop certain characteristics in a plant

cuticle A waxy protective layer on the outside of stems and leaves

dicots Flowering plants that have two embryonic seed leaves

erosion The gradual wearing away of something—usually rock, soil, or land—over a period of time, usually by some natural agent such as water or wind

ethnobiomedical Having to do with the use of plants as medicines in traditional societies

ethnobotany The scientific study of how a traditional society uses plants

extinct (of a species) Having no living members

gametophyte The plant generation produced from spores that produce eggs and sperm

genetic Relating to the passing on of inherited characteristics of an organism

genetically modified (GM) Having to do with organisms that have genetic material that has been artificially altered

germinate To begin to grow and put out shoots after a period of dormancy

gymnosperms Non-flowering seed plants

monocots A group of flowering plants having one seed leaf, vascular tissues arranged throughout the stem, and leaves with parallel veins

organism An individual animal, plant, or other life-form

ovary The organ where eggs are produced

perennial Living for at least two years

petiole The leaf stalk

phloem Vascular tissue that transports nutrients from the leaves to the rest of the plant

photosynthesis The production of sugar and oxygen from carbon dioxide and water in green plants

rhizome An underground horizontal stem that sends out roots and shoots into the soil

specialized Adapted or designed to suit a particular purpose or to perform a specific function

species A group of similar organisms that are capable of exchanging genetic material and breeding; the most individualized classification of a living organism, usually following the group genus and including the name of the genus in its full scientific name

sperm The male sex cell of an organism, usually capable of fertilizing a female sex cell, or egg

spore A tiny unit, often consisting of one cell, that is capable of giving rise to a new individual organism

sporophyte The plant generation produced from eggs and sperm that in turn produces spores

stomata Tiny openings in the leaves and stems of plants that allow gases to enter and leave

thallus The non-vascular body of plants such as liverworts

tissue A group of specialized cells that work together and form the material out of which a living organism is made

tubers Plant structures that are enlarged to store nutrients over the winter or during dry months; also bear buds out of which new plants arise

xylem Vascular tissue that transports water from the roots to the rest of the plant

Further Information

kids.nationalgeographic.com

This site includes amazing plant photographs and fascinating articles about plants all over the planet from National Geographic.

www.bbc.co.uk/nature

Plenty of fun facts about plants and plant habitats can be found on the BBC television Web site. This site is suitable for older readers.

www.newscientist.com

Articles and video clips from *New Scientist* magazine highlight some of the coolest new scientific discoveries.

www.nature.com

The latest scientific research and discoveries from the Web site of *Nature* scientific journal. This site is suitable for older readers.

www.tolweb.org

If you are looking for information about the most current taxonomy of plant species, you will find it here at the Tree of Life Web Project.

www.sciencedaily.com/news/plants_animals

For your daily dose of the latest in scientific discoveries related to plants, check out the images, articles, and video clips on the Science Daily site.

www.sararegistry.gc.ca

To learn more about plants at risk in Canada, you can check out the Species at Risk Public Registry, which includes news, information, and documents on this topic.

www.ntbg.org

The Web site of the National Tropical Botanical Garden in Kauai, Hawaii, has excellent information about tropical plants and Hawaiian lore.

www.globaltrees.org

This Web site contains pictures and scientific information about endangered trees and helpful hints about conservation.

www.eol.org

The Encyclopedia of Life Web site contains photographs and scientific information about a wide variety of plants.

Index

Index

ABOUT THE AUTHORS

Shar Levine and Leslie Johnstone are internationally award-winning, best-selling authors of children's science books and science toys/kits. Leslie Johnstone is also the head of a high school science department. They have written over 50 books and together won the prestigious 2006 Eve Savory Award for Science Communication. Two of their books, *Backyard Science* and *The Ultimate Guide to Your Microscope* were short-listed for the Subaru Prize for hands-on science activity books. Their Web site is www.sciencelady.com, and Shar's blog can also be found on the Web site.